Introduction

Handwriting is an important skill. Acquiring it takes perseverance and practice, whether the writer is left-handed or right-handed. For the left-handed, though, development of the skill of handwriting – in the 'right-handed' world where text runs from left to right – needs just a little more help.

Despite any initial difficulties, with good, regular practice and patient guidance from adults, left-handers can write just as well – and often better – than their right-handed friends. Five to ten minutes of regular daily practice is needed – and this is far more effective than occasional lengthy sessions.

The exercises in this book are intended to be used by the child with adult guidance if necessary. The adult may need to read the instructions to – or with – the child and make sure that the child knows how to form letters and joins correctly, and what to do on the worksheet. For fluent, neat, legible handwriting to develop, it is important for the child from the start to establish accurate letter formation, smooth and consistent joins and even letter sizing.

The child and adult team should therefore work through the book, practising each skill carefully before moving on to the next. The handwriting style in this book has been chosen to help your child write evenly and fluently. However, the child will eventually develop his or her own unique style.

According to the National Handwriting Association, the series is *"... a structured and attractive course that could help a left-hander become a competent, confident writer."* – and which, according to the Head of School Improvement and Achievement, Worcester LEA, *"...will help to improve the writing skills of all left-handers: a valuable resource for teachers and parents."*

squirming   jellyfish

giggling   foxes

Basics for successful skill development

Sit Comfortably

Make sure that the child is sitting in a comfortable position and that the desk or table they are using is not too high. Use a cushion on the seat if necessary. Also, ensure the child has plenty of room so that, if they are working with others, they won't clash elbows with a right-handed neighbour.

Paper Position

It can be helpful for the child to turn their paper – or this book – at an angle. This allows the arm to move freely in line with the hand across the page. Turn the top of the page so that the arrow points directly away from the child and the base of the icon lines up with the edge of the writing table or desk. This will help to develop a consistent working position.

Pen Hold

It is generally acknowledged that the best way to hold a pen or pencil is in the 'tripod' grip, that is, using three fingers. The pen rests on the middle finger and is gripped either side by the thumb and forefinger. The pen should be held about 1.5 cm away from the tip to allow the writing to be seen more clearly. It also keeps the fingers away from the writing. This minimises the likelihood of smudging when the writer is using pen and ink, and it ensures that the fingers are kept above the nib.

Recommended pen hold and paper position.

Gripping a pencil or pen too tightly is a common problem. It will not improve the handwriting and causes the hand to tire quickly. Use of chunky pencils and pencil grips is helpful at an early stage (page 32), as is practice with a marker pen on a whiteboard. Make sure the child turns the board and holds the pen as above, otherwise the child can lift their hand after writing a line to discover a blank board – all the writing has been rubbed off by their hand.

Word Spacing

Correct spacing between words can be a problem for left-handers. Teachers often tell their pupils to "... leave a finger space between words." The child is encouraged to put their finger (a left hand finger is assumed!) at the end of a word and to begin writing the next word immediately after their finger.

This works well for the right-hander but it leaves left-handers doing contortions! Instead, encourage the left-hander to leave the space required for an imaginary letter 'O' between words.

1. Hold your pen correctly.   2. Keep your wrist straight.   3. Don't hold too tight!   **WORKSHEET 1**

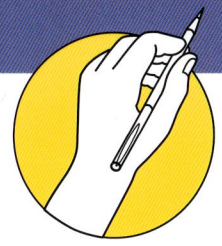

Come with us on a writing journey.
We're going to start in the Stone Age.

Begin by checking your letter formation.

Write over each letter.

a b c d e f g h i j k l m
n o p q r s t u v w x y z
A B C D E F G H I J K L M
N O P Q R S T U V W X Y Z

If you are not sure how to form any of these letters,
check on the letter formation page at the end of this book.

Did you know?
The first kind of writing was in the form of pictures. We call these 'pictograms'.

Turn your paper clockwise. The base of this arrow icon should line up with the edge of your desk.

3

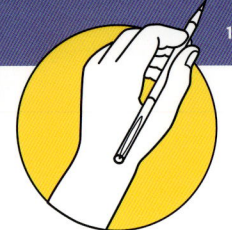

1. Hold your pen correctly.   2. Keep your wrist straight.   3. Don't hold too tight!

WORKSHEET 2

There are four basic letter joins. We will look at these in turn.

This join runs from the base of a letter on the lower dotted line to the next letter at the upper dotted line.

Letter Join 1

ai   ar   un   ur   ir

Trace and complete this letter pattern.

ccccccccccccccccc

Trace and copy these words.

big   pig   dig

mad   bad   lad

Trace and complete this letter pattern.

cacacacacacacaca

Did you know?
The first ever written words were recorded in Iraq, about 5,000 years ago!

The first words were scratched on to wet clay tablets which were then left to dry.

Turn your paper clockwise. The base of this arrow icon should line up with the edge of your desk.

1. Hold your pen correctly.   2. Keep your wrist straight.   3. Don't hold too tight!

WORKSHEET 3

There are four basic letter joins

Letter Join 2

This join starts and finishes on the upper dotted line.

ou   ov   vi   wi   wo

Trace and complete this letter pattern.

oooooooooooooooooooo

Trace and copy these words.

ox   won   wow

These words use joins 1 and 2. Trace and copy them carefully.

cross   crow   cawing

Trace and complete this letter pattern.

ocococococococococ

Did you know? The Egyptians developed a form of pictogram writing called hieroglyphs about 5,000 years ago.

Turn your paper clockwise. The base of this arrow icon should line up with the edge of your desk.

5

1. Hold your pen correctly. 2. Keep your wrist straight. 3. Don't hold too tight!

WORKSHEET 4

There are four basic letter joins

Letter Join 3

This join links the base of a letter to a tall letter.

ab   ul   it   th   bl

Trace and complete this letter pattern.

blblblblblblbl

Trace and copy these words.

all   elk   ebb

These words use joins 1, 2 and 3. Trace and copy them carefully.

slippery   slope   slide

Trace and complete this letter pattern.

ululululululult

Writing developed in different ways all over the world.

Did you know? The Mayan People of Central America developed a pictogram system of their own between 300 and 900 A.D.

Turn your paper clockwise. The base of this arrow icon should line up with the edge of your desk.

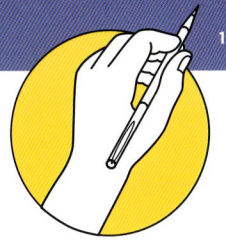

1. Hold your pen correctly. 2. Keep your wrist straight. 3. Don't hold too tight!

WORKSHEET 5

There are four basic letter joins

Letter Join 4

This join begins on the upper dotted line, linking one letter to a tall letter.

ot   rt   ob   rk   wl

The Chinese invented paper.

Trace and complete this letter pattern.

rkrkrkrkrkrk

These words use joins 1, 2 and 4. Trace and copy them carefully.

howl   bark   whine

Have a go at completing these patterns.

Aiya!

Did you know? The Arabs learnt the secret of paper-making from Chinese prisoners of war in 768 A.D.

Turn your paper clockwise. The base of this arrow icon should line up with the edge of your desk.

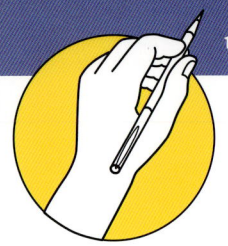

1. Hold your pen correctly. 2. Keep your wrist straight. 3. Don't hold too tight!

WORKSHEET 6

Here are some special joins.

The letter 'f' is never joined from the letter before it.
The crossbar of the 'f' joins to the next letter... unless it's an 'e'.

Trace and copy these words.

Go on, try saying these words quickly!

When there are two letter 'f's together,
write them both then add the cross bar.

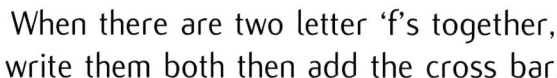

> **Did you know?** An octopus squirts ink when it is alarmed.

When an 'f' is followed by a 't'
join the 'f' to the 't'
and then add the cross bar to the 't'
after you've finished writing the word.

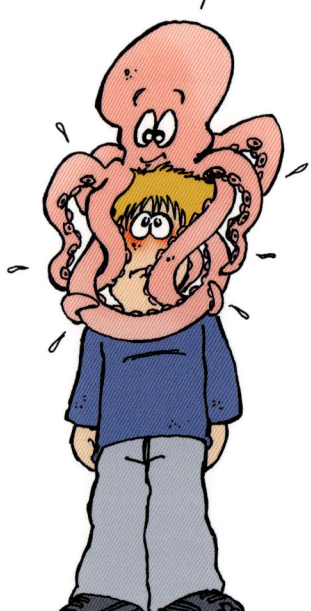

I wonder if anyone has ever tried writing with octopus ink!

Trace and copy this sentence.

The life raft drifted after the ship.

Turn your paper clockwise. The base of this arrow icon should line up with the edge of your desk.

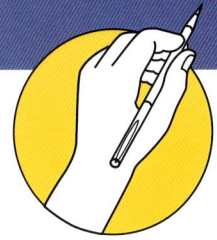

1. Hold your pen correctly. 2. Keep your wrist straight. 3. Don't hold too tight!

WORKSHEET 7

Here are some more special joins.

The letter 'z' is never joined from the letter before it, but it does join to the next letter.

ze

Copy and trace these words.

zany   zebras   dozing   lazily

The letters 'g', 'j', 'q', 'y' and 'x' can be joined from the letter before them, but they don't like to join the next letter.
It's best to take your pen or pencil off the paper
when you've written one of these letters and then begin the next letter.

go   jo   qu   xi   yo

Copy and trace these words.

squirming   jellyfish   giggling   foxes

Did you know?
Before paper was invented, people wrote on stones, pottery, bamboo, reeds and even animal skin.

Turn your paper clockwise. The base of this arrow icon should line up with the edge of your desk.

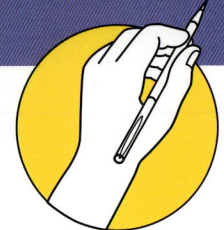

1. Hold your pen correctly. 2. Keep your wrist straight. 3. Don't hold too tight!

WORKSHEET 8

The Chinese
developed a writing system all of their own.

Trace and copy the menu.

THE BAMBOO GARDEN MENU

STARTER
Chicken Noodle Soup

MAIN COURSE
Vegetable Chow Mein

Crispy Prawn Crackers

DESSERT
Pineapple Fritter

Did you know? Chinese characters are written one underneath the other in columns.

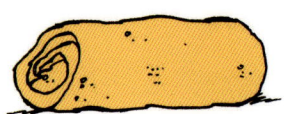

Turn your paper clockwise. The base of this arrow icon should line up with the edge of your desk.

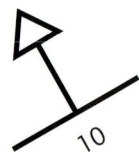

1. Hold your pen correctly. 2. Keep your wrist straight. 3. Don't hold too tight!   **WORKSHEET 9**

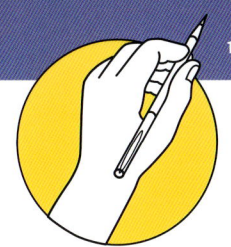

Chinese writing is made up of characters that stand for a word or idea rather than a single letter. Each character is made up of as many as 26 different strokes which must be written in the correct order. Phew!

Did you know? There are over 50,000 Chinese characters!

Now write your own international menu.
Choose any food you like.

Tomato Soup   Garlic Bread

Starter:
_____
_____
_____

Chocolate Mousse   Baked Beans   Melon

Main Course:
_____
_____
_____

Peas   Rice

Treacle Tart   Strawberry Ice Cream

Dessert:
_____
_____

Spaghetti Bolognaise   Chicken Curry   Chips   Cheese and Tomato Pizza

Turn your paper clockwise. The base of this arrow icon should line up with the edge of your desk.

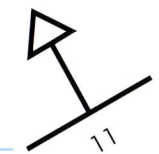

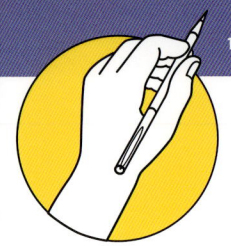

1. Hold your pen correctly.   2. Keep your wrist straight.   3. Don't hold too tight!

WORKSHEET 10

The first alphabet was used around 2000 B.C.
This alphabet developed into all the alphabets used today. There are lots of different alphabets, for example, Roman, Greek and Cyrillic (upon which the Russian alphabet is based).

Trace and copy these Latin phrases and their meanings.
How many do you know?

Vice versa – the other way round

Terra firma – solid ground

TERRA VERY FIRMA !

Ad infinitum – endlessly

Did you know?
The alphabet we use for English is the Roman alphabet. The Ancient Romans used it for their Latin language.

Turn your paper clockwise. The base of this arrow icon should line up with the edge of your desk.

1. Hold your pen correctly. 2. Keep your wrist straight. 3. Don't hold too tight!   **WORKSHEET 11**

Caesar and Calphurnia have been shopping at the market place. Below are all the things they bought.

Trace Caesar's list

and then write the rest of the items on Calphurnia's list.

CAESAR   CALPHURNIA

Complete the pattern above.

TURN YOUR PAPER CLOCKWISE. THE BASE OF THIS ARROW ICON SHOULD LINE UP WITH THE EDGE OF YOUR DESK.

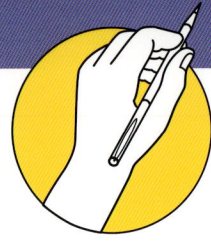

1. Hold your pen correctly.   2. Keep your wrist straight.   3. Don't hold too tight!

WORKSHEET 12

IN MEDIEVAL TIMES MANY PEOPLE COULD NOT READ OR WRITE. PEOPLE WHO WERE EMPLOYED TO WRITE WERE CALLED SCRIBES.

Did you know?
Until printing was invented in the 15th Century every book had to be written by hand!

Trace and copy this letter.

My dearest Guinevere,

Thank thee kindly for the

woolly socks knitted by

thine own fair hand.

from thy true love,
Sir Spearalot

Did you know?
Scribes used crushed beetles to make red ink!

Complete this pattern.

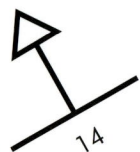

TURN YOUR PAPER CLOCKWISE. THE BASE OF THIS ARROW ICON SHOULD LINE UP WITH THE EDGE OF YOUR DESK.

1. Hold your pen correctly. 2. Keep your wrist straight. 3. Don't hold too tight! **WORKSHEET 13**

Medieval scribes wrote with large bird feathers called quills.

Did you know?
Bird feathers curve – which means the feathers from the right wing of a large bird are best for left-handers!

Now write your own letter.
Use the words around the page or your own ideas.
Try to use every line.

Uncle Bill
Sybil
I'm writing to ask
if you would like to
come swimming
go to a party

Dear

Mr Brown
Thank you for
the nice jumper
the computer game
the chocolates
Let's meet at half-past two

from   Yours sincerely,
Did you enjoy your holiday?   See you soon.   With lots of love,
It's great!   With best wishes,

Turn your paper clockwise. The base of this arrow icon should line up with the edge of your desk.

1. Hold your pen correctly.   2. Keep your wrist straight.   3. Don't hold too tight!

WORKSHEET 14

THE CELTS WERE TRIBAL PEOPLE FROM THE EARLY MIDDLE AGES. THEY ARE MOST REMEMBERED FOR THEIR BEAUTIFUL ILLUMINATED MANUSCRIPTS. SOME OF THESE CAN STILL BE SEEN IN MUSEUMS TODAY.

Copy this rhyme.

Arthur was a Celtic king

The Anglo-Saxons feared him,

He battled with his fearless knights,

Who scattered all against them.

Did you know? 'ILLUMINATED' MEANS THE WRITING IS DECORATED IN GOLD AND OTHER COLOURS. THE CELTS ADDED EXTRA PICTURES AND DESIGNS TO THEIR WRITING.

Trace and complete this letter pattern.

urururururur

TURN YOUR PAPER CLOCKWISE. THE BASE OF THIS ARROW ICON SHOULD LINE UP WITH THE EDGE OF YOUR DESK.

16

1. Hold your pen correctly.   2. Keep your wrist straight.   3. Don't hold too tight!   **WORKSHEET 15**

TRY SOME CELTIC WRITING OF YOUR OWN...

Tape two pencils together so that the left is slightly shorter than the right.
(If your right-handed friends want to do this they will have to do it
the other way round.)

Try writing some large round letters.

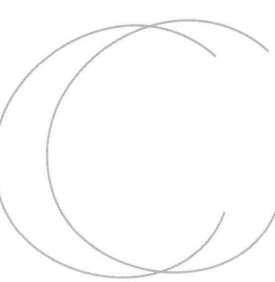
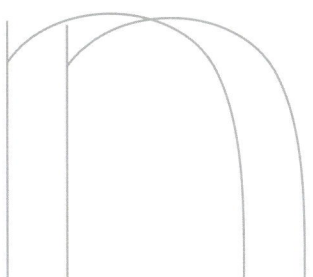

Join the 'loose' ends and colour in with a black pen.
Try adding some spirals.

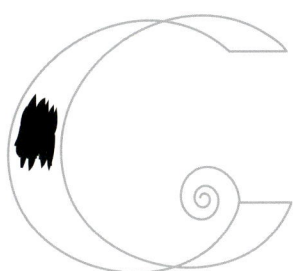
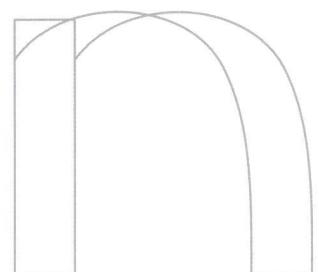

Here is Pat's name.
Finish the pattern around his name.

Now try writing your own name in a Celtic script.
If you use a piece of card, you could make it into a label for your door!

Turn your paper clockwise. The base of this arrow icon should line up with the edge of your desk.

1. Hold your pen correctly. 2. Keep your wrist straight. 3. Don't hold too tight!

WORKSHEET 16

Copy this invitation.

The Court of King John

cordially invites thee

to the feast of St Stephen.

Bring thine own platter.

Did you know?
Envelopes weren't used until the 19th Century. Before then, letters were simply folded up and sometimes sealed with sealing wax.

Copy this letter pattern.

aeaeaeae

Turn your paper clockwise. The base of this arrow icon should line up with the edge of your desk.

1. Hold your pen correctly. 2. Keep your wrist straight. 3. Don't hold too tight!

WORKSHEET 17

Now write your own invitation.
Use the words around the page to help you, or write your own ideas.

Name

Would like to invite

Name

To a

On

Please

RSVP

On Friday 31st October   Please bring a pumpkin
To a birthday party   Please wear smart clothes
On Saturday 12th August   To a Halloween party

Mr and Mrs Brown

Please wear fancy dress

To the wedding of

Did you know? RSVP is a French abbreviation: 'Répondez s'il vous plaît' which means 'please reply'.

Complete this pattern.

Turn your paper clockwise. The base of this arrow icon should line up with the edge of your desk.

1. Hold your pen correctly. 2. Keep your wrist straight. 3. Don't hold too tight!

WORKSHEET 18

Copy this recipe.

Ye old recipe – Mutton Stew

Heat potful of stock on fire.

Add pieces of raw mutton.

Toss in sprigs of rosemary.

Add flagon of cider.

Simmer all morning.

Serve on a platter.

TURN YOUR PAPER CLOCKWISE. THE BASE OF THIS ARROW ICON SHOULD LINE UP WITH THE EDGE OF YOUR DESK.

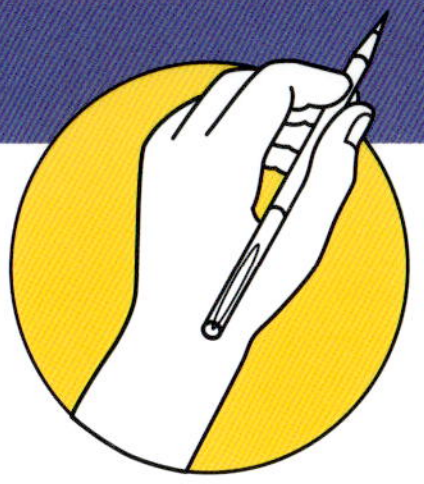

1. Hold your pen correctly.   2. Keep your wrist straight.   3. Don't hold too tight!

WORKSHEET 19

Trace and complete this pizza recipe and fill in the missing words.

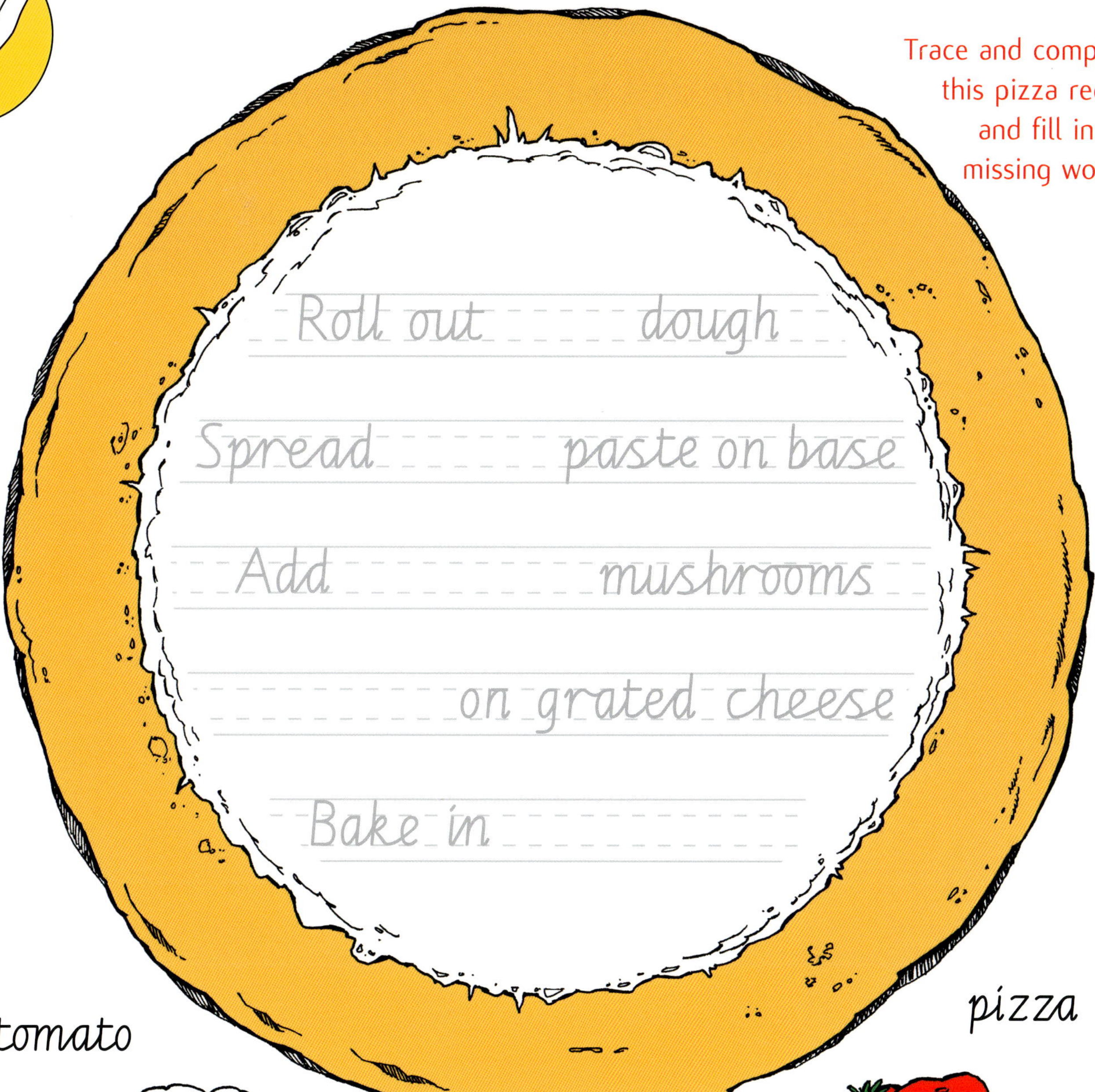

Roll out _____ dough

Spread _____ paste on base

Add _____ mushrooms

_____ on grated cheese

Bake in _____

tomato

Sprinkle

sliced

pizza

oven

Trace and complete this pattern.

kekeke

TURN YOUR PAPER CLOCKWISE. THE BASE OF THIS ARROW ICON SHOULD LINE UP WITH THE EDGE OF YOUR DESK.

1. Hold your pen correctly. 2. Keep your wrist straight. 3. Don't hold too tight!   **WORKSHEET 20**

Leonardo da Vinci was a 15th Century artist and inventor. He is a famous left-hander. He wrote many of his notes in 'mirror-writing' (starting at the right and writing backwards towards the left hand side of the page).

Did you know? Arabic is written from the right hand side to the left.

Someone has been to Paris. Can you read who?

Trace and copy his postcard.

Dear Joe

Yesterday, I went to the Louvre.

I saw the Mona Lisa.

See you soon, Leonardo (mirror-writing)

Did you know? Some left-handers are good at mirror-writing. It's a good way of making your diary difficult for other people to read.

Did you know? Some people can write or draw with both hands at the same time!

Trace and complete this letter pattern.

nonono

Turn your paper clockwise. The base of this arrow icon should line up with the edge of your desk.

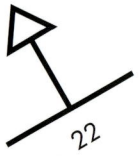

1. Hold your pen correctly. 2. Keep your wrist straight. 3. Don't hold too tight!   **WORKSHEET 21**

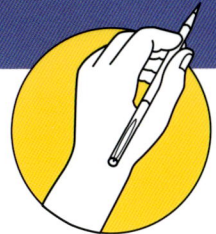

Here is Joe's address.

Copy Joe's Address.

Mr J Hall
36 Greenfield Avenue,

Stratford-upon-Avon,

Warwickshire.

Now write your own address.

House number and street name

Town or city

County (or State)

Do you know your postcode (or Zip Code)?

Turn your paper clockwise. The base of this arrow icon should line up with the edge of your desk.

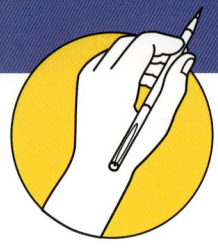

1. Hold your pen correctly. 2. Keep your wrist straight. 3. Don't hold too tight!

WORKSHEET 22

Now write your own personal fact file.
Fill in these facts using the words below, or by making up your own.

Name:

Hair colour:

Eye colour:

Hobbies:

Favourite foods:

Dislikes:

Cycling

Spinach   Brown   Playing chess   Listening to music
Spaghetti   Pizza   Sewing
Blonde   Baked beans   Green
Tomatoes   Skipping   Playing football
Red   Painting
Reading   Skateboarding   Rock climbing   Blue

TURN YOUR PAPER CLOCKWISE. THE BASE OF THIS ARROW ICON SHOULD LINE UP WITH THE EDGE OF YOUR DESK.

24

1. Hold your pen correctly. **2.** Keep your wrist straight. **3.** Don't hold too tight!

WORKSHEET 23

Pencils have been around since the 16th Century.

Copy the pencil-making instructions.

Mix graphite powder with clay.

Roll into a long thin bar. Fire in a kiln.

Dip into wax. Put the thin bar into a groove cut into a piece of wood and glue another piece of wood on top.

Did you know?
The first pencils were made from graphite found in Cumbria in Northern England. The graphite was used for marking sheep.

Turn your paper clockwise. The base of this arrow icon should line up with the edge of your desk.

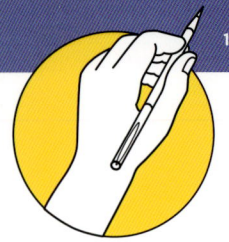

1. Hold your pen correctly.   2. Keep your wrist straight.   3. Don't hold too tight!

WORKSHEET 24

Victorian children had to practise their writing in 'copybooks'.

They learnt to write in a 'copperplate' handwriting style.
They copied out a sentence many times, usually a proverb or a piece of useful information.
They were very careful not to 'blot their copybook'.

Copy these proverbs.

Birds of a feather flock together.

Great oaks from little acorns grow.

Time and tide wait for no man.

Two heads are better than one.

Did you know?
Until the 1970's school desks each had a small inkwell in them for pupils to dip their pens into.

Turn your paper clockwise. The base of this arrow icon should line up with the edge of your desk.

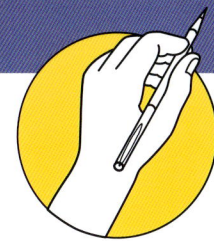

1. Hold your pen correctly. 2. Keep your wrist straight. 3. Don't hold too tight!

WORKSHEET 25

The Minoans were Bronze Age people

living on the island of Crete. They led a very civilised life. They had a written language which we call 'Linear A'. Archaeologists have still not managed to decipher it. 'Linear A' gradually changed into a new written language called 'Linear B'. This was deciphered in 1952 by a British architect, Michael Ventris.

Copy this information.

Samuel Morse developed a method of sending a code of dots and dashes by electric telegraph.

It was used at sea until 1993.

Did you know? A cipher is a secret code or the key to a code. Morse Code is a cipher. It was invented by an American, Samuel Morse, in 1844.

Did you know? SOS is a distress call used at sea and comes from the Morse Code signal.

Turn your paper clockwise. The base of this arrow icon should line up with the edge of your desk.

1. Hold your pen correctly. 2. Keep your wrist straight. 3. Don't hold too tight!

WORKSHEET 26

DURING WORLD WAR TWO, THE GERMANS INVENTED A MACHINE CALLED ENIGMA TO MAKE CODED MESSAGES WHICH THEY THOUGHT WOULD NEVER BE DECIPHERED. POLISH AND BRITISH MATHEMATICIANS EVENTUALLY CRACKED THIS CODE.

Copy these messages.

Meet in the cafe at ten past two.

Look out for a man with a dog.

Pass this message to the guard.

Use the alphabet on the side of the page to crack this message.

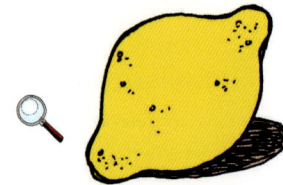

Did you know?
Spies often used invisible ink for their messages. You can make your own with lemon juice. When the message has faded it can be revealed by careful ironing.

Turn your paper clockwise. The base of this arrow icon should line up with the edge of your desk.

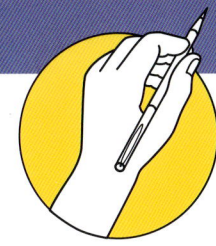

1. Hold your pen correctly.   2. Keep your wrist straight.   3. Don't hold too tight!

WORKSHEET 27

Handwriting is one of the most important inventions ever.

Most of what we know about the past comes from written records. Even in this electronic age, handwriting is a useful skill. A person's handwriting is unique. Some official documents are still handwritten.

> **Did you know?** A man called Samuel Pepys kept a diary from 1660 to 1669. He described the Fire of London and the Great Plague amongst other things. He wrote his diary in code. It was deciphered in 1825.

Copy Samuel Pepys' diary entry.

3rd September 1666

I woke in the night to the sound of

people running and shouting.

There was a terrible smell of smoke.

Samuel Pepys

SAMUEL PEPYS

Turn your paper clockwise. The base of this arrow icon should line up with the edge of your desk.

29

1. Hold your pen correctly. 2. Keep your wrist straight. 3. Don't hold too tight!

PRACTICE SHEET

Use this page for more practice.

Turn your paper clockwise. The base of this arrow icon should line up with the edge of your desk.

REFERENCE SHEET

a b c d e f g
h i j k l m n
o p q r s t u
v w x y z

Use this page as a handy reference.

REFERENCE SHEET

1 2 3 4 5

6 7 8 9 0

Use this page as a handy reference.

REFERENCE SHEET

Use this page as a handy reference.

More help for left-handers

Many products have been designed for use with the left hand. There are also specialist centres which offer advice for left-handers, their parents and teachers, and which supply products for left-handed use. Some of the items which relate to activities in this book are described below, but there are many other invaluable everyday devices available for both children and adults. These range from sloping desks to can openers, scissors to secateurs and even golf clubs and electric guitars. A few of the centres around the world which supply products for left-handers, or offer educational advice on left-handed issues, are listed below.

A DVD entitled *Left-Handed Children – A Guide for Teachers and Parents*, by the authors of this series and endorsed by the Teacher Training Agency, is available via the authors' own website – *leftshoponline.co.uk* – which also carries details of the teacher training workshops provided by Mark Stewart.

Educational Products

Pens

There are a number of ink pens which can be useful for left-handers. A good technique and appropriate pen make writing a much more pleasurable experience.

Stabilo produces an excellent pen called the EASYoriginal Graffiti. Make sure you get the 'Graffiti' version! It has the grip moulded into the barrel, like the EASYergo pencil by the same company. This pen helps to maintain the same dynamic tripod grip throughout your child's school life.

With the EASYoriginal Graffiti, each time a new cartridge is inserted a new nib is automatically introduced. The ink can also be erased.

Schneider has also produced a very useful pen. It has a rollerball nib but uses ordinary ink cartridges. It also has a tripod grip. This is a great pen for school use.

Italic Pens and Pens for Calligraphy

Manuscript produces pens and calligraphy sets designed for the technique where the hand comes from under the writing, not smudging or hook styles. They require a precise technique for effective use, making handwriting an interesting hobby.

Scissors

These can be right- or left-handed, **not** both. Proper left-handed scissors have the blades set so that, when held either way up in the left hand, the cutting edge is clearly visible on the inside of the scissors. Not being able to use scissors, particularly at a young age, can cause frustration and loss of self-esteem.

Rulers

Left-handed rulers have the scale running from right to left, which allows the left-hander to pull the pencil rather than pushing and going away from the scale rather than obscuring it!

Sharpeners

There are left-handed pencil sharpeners. These are held in the right hand, and the pencil is turned away from the body. Usually with two holes, the larger hole offers reasonable sharpening for triangular pencils.

Further Reading

The Left-hander's Handbook by Diane G Paul
Published by Robinswood Press.
ISBN 978-1906053-819

So You Think They're Left-Handed?
by Mark and Heather Stewart
Published by Robinswood Press.
ISBN 978-1906053-956